CW01064628

Original title:
The Architect's Muse

Author: Thor Castlebury
ISBN HARDBACK: 978-9916-88-090-6
ISBN PAPERBACK: 978-9916-88-091-3

Elysian Edifices

In the realm where dreams reside,
Marble towers touch the sky,
Gilded halls with whispers glide,
Time stands still, as hopes fly.

Gardens bloom with colors bright,
Rivers sing a soft refrain,
Stars will watch through velvet night,
Joy and peace to ever reign.

Echoes of the past will call,
Through the mist, a story flows,
Every heart, it shall enthrall,
In this land, love only grows.

Hearts rejoicing, spirits free,
In the glow of twilight's grace,
Elysian beauty, come and see,
In these edifices, find your place.

Frames of Freedom

In the dawn's gentle light,
Dreams take flight, so bright.
Every moment we chase,
In this vast, open space.

Hearts unbound, we roam,
Finding solace in home.
With each step we find,
The peace of the mind.

Scale of Serenity

Upon the mountains high,
Whispers of wind sigh.
Nature's calm embrace,
Fills time's empty space.

With each note of the stream,
Life flows like a dream.
Soft shadows align,
In this moment divine.

Silhouettes Against the Sky

As the sun starts to fade,
Figures dance in the glade.
In the twilight they play,
Chasing shadows away.

Colors blend into night,
Stars begin their flight.
A canvas unfolds wide,
With the moon as our guide.

Serendipity in Structure

In the chaos of life,
Beauty cuts through the strife.
Patterns emerge so clear,
In the moments we steer.

Each stumble, a chance found,
With laughter resound.
Through the maze we flow,
Seeking treasures below.

Illumination in Design

In shadows cast by forms unknown,
Bright visions rise, in colors grown.
Shapes entwine and dance with grace,
Their brilliance finds a cherished space.

Each pattern tells a story true,
Of dreams entwined in vibrant hue.
With every line, a thought expressed,
A legacy in art is blessed.

Sculpting the Ethereal

Glimmers caught in morning's light,
Soft whispers born of pure delight.
Crafting forms that touch the sky,
With every stroke, the spirits fly.

Chiseled grace in stone's embrace,
A fleeting moment, time's own trace.
Transcending boundaries, they reveal,
The beauty found in what we feel.

Threads of Thought

A tapestry of woven dreams,
Each strand connects, or so it seems.
With every knot, a tale entwined,
In colors bright, the heart aligned.

The mind's design in fabric's weave,
Stories linger, then they leave.
Yet in the silence, we still find,
The echoes of the threads combined.

Harmonizing Homesteads

Within the walls, a warmth resides,
Where laughter blooms and joy abides.
Each corner holds a treasured space,
A refuge filled with love and grace.

Nature's touch frames every view,
In gentleness, the world feels new.
Together in this sacred place,
We craft our dreams, our hearts embrace.

Inspiration in Stillness

In quiet corners, thoughts arise,
The world slows down, the spirit flies.
Moments linger, softly bare,
In stillness, find what's truly there.

Glimmers of light dance in the mind,
Nature whispers, calm and kind.
With every breath, the heart beats low,
In silence, inner truths will flow.

Masonry of Emotion

Brick by brick, our feelings lay,
Constructing walls, come what may.
With every tear, a story grows,
Each joy, a window, love bestows.

Strong foundations built on trust,
In every heart, we find the rust.
Mortar mixed with laughter's sound,
In this realm, our souls are bound.

The Craft of Shadows

In twilight's hue, soft shadows play,
Crafting stories in shades of gray.
Each flicker holds a hidden fear,
In the dim light, we draw near.

Figures dance with whispered grace,
In silence, we each find our place.
Illusions weave a gentle shroud,
In the darkness, we are proud.

Buildings of Belief

Tall spires rising, reaching high,
Faith constructed toward the sky.
With every doubt, we lay a stone,
In unity, we're never alone.

Windows open, visions bright,
Together, we ignite the night.
Each heartbeat echoes through the halls,
In these buildings, love never falls.

Designs in the Ether

In the veil of twilight's glow,
Shapes begin to softly flow.
Whispers of the night's design,
Crafted dreams, both yours and mine.

Clouds weave tales of silent grace,
Drawing lines in endless space.
Stars like ink on velvet spread,
Sketching thoughts we all have bred.

Fractals dance in cosmic fire,
Glimmers of a shared desire.
In the fabric of the night,
We find peace, we find our light.

The Pulse of Construction

Rumbling engines, clattering steel,
The city's heart begins to feel.
Foundations laid, a structure born,
In dreams of heights, we push the dawn.

Brick by brick, the vision stands,
Crafted by skilled, steady hands.
Laughter echoes, toil entwined,
In every corner, hope designed.

As daylight fades, the lights ignite,
A bustling scene, a vibrant sight.
Here, ambition meets the ground,
In every pulse, progress found.

Transitions of Thought

Ideas flicker, then ignite,
As shadows dance in fading light.
Moments captured, times collide,
In the depths where secrets hide.

Waves of change begin to flow,
Carving paths where few dare go.
With every thought, a bridge we make,
Transforming dreams with each heartache.

Connections form in silken threads,
Weaving stories, as life spreads.
In this tapestry of mind,
The truth in us, we seek to find.

A Journey through Junctions

Crossroads beckon, paths diverge,
In every choice, a silent surge.
Maps of fate lay before our eyes,
In every turn, a new surprise.

Voices call from every lane,
Reminders of joy and pain.
Each step carries weight and grace,
In every heart, a sacred space.

As the compass swings and spins,
We gather wisdom from our sins.
Through junctions wide and narrow flows,
A journey rich, where spirit grows.

Dreams in the Dust

Whispers in the twilight, fade,
Fleeting wishes linger, made.
Stardust trails on silent nights,
Lost in shadows, fleeting lights.

Footprints mark the paths we tread,
Echoes of the words we said.
In the silence, hope remains,
Dreams await through joy and pains.

Time, a river flowing fast,
Holds the moments of the past.
In the dust, our visions stir,
In the quiet, dreams confer.

Fractured light through gentle haze,
Hints of magic in the maze.
Dancing figures shift and sway,
Dreams in dust, they softly play.

Frame of Heartbeat

In the stillness, pulses race,
Every moment, find your place.
Time a canvas, love the hue,
Frame the heartbeat, pure and true.

Whispers drift through morning light,
Tender sighs that hold us tight.
Captured glances, fleeting fate,
Frame of heartbeat, never wait.

Colors blend in twilight's glow,
Gather feelings, let them flow.
In each rhythm, find your song,
Frame the heartbeat, where we belong.

Echoes dance through every breath,
Life a tapestry of depth.
In the silence, hearts ignite,
Frame of heartbeat, love's delight.

Lattice of Longing

Threads of yearning weave through time,
Dreams entwined in silent rhyme.
Caught in webs of hopes and fears,
Lattice strong, yet fragile tears.

In the shadows, hearts collide,
Whispers soft, yet bold inside.
Through the lattice, visions blend,
Longing grows, a faithful friend.

Moments linger, sweet and rare,
Breathless whispers fill the air.
In each touch and fleeting glance,
Lattice of longing, woven chance.

Boundless space, yet close they stand,
Fingers touch, a gentle hand.
Within the weave, our dreams take flight,
Lattice of longing, day and night.

Columns of Contemplation

Beneath the arches, thoughts arise,
Silent whispers, timeless sighs.
Columns strong, they hold the weight,
In contemplation, hearts await.

Every question finds its voice,
In the stillness, we rejoice.
Echoes dance on ancient stone,
Guiding minds to the unknown.

Reflections in the gentle light,
Carved from shadows, bold and bright.
In the stillness, wisdom flows,
Columns stand, where silence grows.

Through the ages, stories weave,
Embers of the past, we grieve.
In each pause, we find a way,
Columns of contemplation, stay.

Blueprints of Inspiration

Lines of thought on paper flow,
Sketches born from dreams we know.
Every curve and angle shines,
Crafting futures from designs.

In the quiet, visions spark,
Ideas light the canvas dark.
With each stroke, our passions rise,
Building castles in the skies.

Hands that shape the worlds we see,
Mapping out our destiny.
Chasing shadows, drawing light,
Blueprints guide us through the night.

From the chaos, order grows,
Inspiration's fire glows.
Each creation, a bold stance,
In this dance of life, we prance.

Foundations of Reverie

Beneath the dreamer's gentle sigh,
Foundations set to reach the sky.
Quiet thoughts like whispers speak,
Building realms where spirits seek.

Waves of wonder, tides of grace,
In this space, we find our place.
From the earth, our visions bloom,
Lifting hopes above the gloom.

Crafted dreams both near and far,
Shining brighter than a star.
Sturdy beams of hope and light,
Hold our dreams both day and night.

In reverie, we stake our claim,
Each foundation, a spark of flame.
With every thought, our spirits rise,
Building worlds beyond the skies.

Whispers in the Blueprint

In the margins, secrets hide,
Whispers soft, our dreams abide.
Every mark a thought released,
In the silence, visions feast.

Gentle breezes carry plans,
Dancing lightly with our hands.
Sketches pulse with life anew,
Lost in dreams, we find what's true.

On the page, a story told,
Crafting futures, brave and bold.
In each line, a spark ignites,
Guiding us to lofty heights.

Through the whispers, echoes play,
Guiding hearts along the way.
In the blueprint, hopes align,
Crafting paths, your hand in mine.

Dreams Through Drafts

Drafts adorned with visions bright,
Chasing shadows into light.
Every line a tale unfolds,
Whispers of what could be told.

In the drafting room we gather,
Where ideas flow and doubts shatter.
With each stroke, we carve our fate,
Turning dreams to something great.

Papers crumpled, thoughts reborn,
In every failure, hope is worn.
Through the drafts, we stitch our fate,
Finding magic, never late.

From the chaos, beauty springs,
In our hearts, the freedom sings.
Dreams through drafts, our voices soar,
Building dreams forevermore.

Sunlit Schematics

In gentle rays the morning glows,
Colors burst where the garden grows.
Leaves dance lightly in warm embrace,
Nature's art, a sacred space.

Blue skies cradle the golden hue,
Winding paths that lead to you.
Whispers soft as a summer breeze,
Capture hearts with subtle ease.

Sunflowers tilt to greet the sun,
Every moment a joy begun.
Patterns drawn in shadows play,
Map the night and greet the day.

In this light, our dreams take flight,
Guided by the stars at night.
Underneath the vast expanse,
Life unfolds, a sweet romance.

Renderings of Desire

Crimson lips and whispering sighs,
In your gaze, my wild heart flies.
With every brush of velvet skin,
A world awakens deep within.

Silken threads of longing weave,
In the night, we dare believe.
Passion flares with each soft touch,
Creating flames that mean so much.

In the silence, our souls collide,
A journey taken side by side.
Hearts entwined like vines that cling,
To the melody our bodies sing.

Promises painted in the dark,
Elements dance, a vital spark.
In the echo of sweet embrace,
Desire finds its truest place.

The Symmetry of Dreams

In twilight's glow, our visions blend,
Ethereal paths where wishes send.
We sail on clouds, so soft, so light,
Chasing shadows that dance in flight.

Mirrored thoughts in silent streams,
Reflecting depths of vibrant dreams.
Every heartbeat a subtle sign,
Connecting realms where stars align.

In whispered hopes, we find our way,
Guided by the moon's soft sway.
Echoes of laughter fill the air,
Beneath the night, we shed our care.

The universe, a canvas wide,
Colors our souls, the dreams abide.
In this symmetry, we stand clear,
Unity found, forever near.

Foundations of Feeling

Roots that tether in shared ground,
Time weaves stories all around.
From tangled paths, our hearts will grow,
Strong as the winds that softly blow.

With every glance, the world ignites,
Building bridges through starry nights.
Hands entwined, we craft our place,
Foundations set in love's embrace.

In whispered vows, our truths reside,
A sanctuary where hearts confide.
Waves of trust that rise and fall,
Carrying dreams to answer the call.

Through storms and calm, we'll stand together,
Fortified by each shared tether.
In every feeling, pure and strong,
We find the beat to our own song.

Skylines of the Soul

Across the city, dreams do rise,
In every shadow, hope implies.
The skyline stretches far and wide,
An arch of passion, hearts in stride.

In every window, stories glow,
A silent dance of ebb and flow.
Each brick a tale, a whispered oath,
United souls, embracing growth.

With every dawn, new journeys start,
The skyline speaks, igniting art.
A canvas high where visions soar,
The soul's reflection, evermore.

As twilight dims and stars appear,
The city hums, a song sincere.
In every heart, a skyline waits,
A treasure found, love's open gates.

Blueprints of Inspiration

On paper lies a dream begun,
With careful lines, the vision runs.
A sketch of life, of hopes anew,
In every curve, the heart breaks through.

The architect of thoughts so grand,
Constructing futures, hand in hand.
With pencil's touch, the world does smile,
In every blueprint, dreams compile.

Each angle sharp, each space defined,
Inspiration flows, entwined, aligned.
With every stroke, a story clear,
The plans unfold, the path appears.

In shadows cast by visions bright,
The blueprints guide us through the night.
Through twists and turns, the heart will lead,
Creating wonders, planting seed.

Structures of the Soul

In frames of steel and hopes of gold,
Structures rise, both brave and bold.
Each beam a strength, a story told,
In harmony, as dreams unfold.

Foundations deep, like roots of trees,
A structure built to brave the breeze.
With every choice, a heart aligns,
Creating spaces where love shines.

Windows wide to let light stream,
In every corner, visions gleam.
The soul constructs its inner space,
A sanctuary, a warm embrace.

Through storms and trials, it stands tall,
The structure of the soul, through all.
In every heart, the architect,
Learns to build and to protect.

Whispers of the Design

In gentle tones, the whispers call,
A design woven through it all.
With every breath, the patterns weave,
In artful grace, we dare believe.

The silence speaks in curves and lines,
A language deep where beauty shines.
With every thought, a story's spun,
In whispers soft, the heart is won.

As colors blend, a canvas bright,
The design of life takes flight.
In every detail, secrets hum,
A melody of dreams to come.

Through night and day, the whispers play,
Unraveling truths along the way.
In every heart, the design persists,
Whispers of fate, in love's sweet twists.

Crafting the Cosmos

Stars align in endless night,
Dreams take flight in cosmic light.
Galaxies swirl with tender grace,
In this vast and boundless space.

Waves of time, a flowing stream,
Creating worlds within a dream.
Nebulas whisper in colors bright,
Painting the canvas of our sight.

From stardust we rise and roam,
In the universe we find our home.
Each heartbeat, a rhythm divine,
Crafting the cosmos, your hand in mine.

Infinite patterns, woven tight,
In the tapestry of the night.
Every moment, a spark, a dare,
Crafting the cosmos, a love affair.

Mosaic of the Mind

Thoughts collide, a vibrant dance,
Fragments fused in happenstance.
Colorful shards, a vivid blend,
In the mind, where stories end.

Whispers echo, dreams take form,
Ideas shift, a restless storm.
Each piece tells its tale, refined,
Building the mosaic of the mind.

Images crash, emotions stream,
In this chaos, we find a gleam.
Past and future intertwine, so bold,
A treasure chest of stories untold.

Curious hearts seek to explore,
Each mosaic opens a door.
In shattered glass, beauty defined,
Crafting a mosaic of the mind.

Shadows of Silhouette

Silhouettes dance in fading light,
Casting dreams into the night.
Moments linger, echoes fade,
In the twilight, memories made.

Whispers wrap around the soul,
In shadows soft, we feel whole.
The night unfolds its quiet art,
Shadows of silhouette, where we start.

Figures drift on silver streams,
Lost in the fabric of our dreams.
Each shape a story, a secret told,
Shadows watching as life unfolds.

As dawn approaches, shadows yield,
Revealing truths that were concealed.
In fleeting forms, we trace the thread,
Shadows of silhouette, where we are led.

Lines of Lament

Ink flows freely, thoughts aflame,
Lines of lament, heartache named.
Words wound softly, bittersweet,
In this silence, sorrow meets.

Each stroke a tear, a whispered sigh,
Beneath the weight of the sky.
Memory echoes through the pen,
Lines of lament, again and again.

Pages worn with tales of grief,
Finding solace in belief.
Ink-bound tears, a cathartic spree,
Lines of lament set us free.

In every word, a story lies,
Tracing the pain, the whispered why's.
Through the verses, we rise and mend,
Lines of lament, a friend till the end.

Canopy of Creation

Beneath the vast sky's embrace,
Leaves whisper secrets with grace.
Branches cradle dreams alive,
In nature's heart, we thrive.

Sunlight dapples the forest floor,
Painting shadows, a vibrant lore.
Each creature sings its own song,
In harmony, we all belong.

Clouds drift lazily from afar,
Guiding wanderers like a star.
The breeze carries tales untold,
In this realm, magic unfolds.

Edges of Enchantment

In twilight's glow, the world transforms,
Mysteries dance in swirling forms.
Stars awaken from their slumber,
Revealing secrets, a sweet wonder.

Moonlight bathes the night in gold,
Whispers of stories yet to be told.
The air is thick with dreams in flight,
As shadows weave through soft twilight.

Enchanting echoes in the trees,
Swaying gently with the breeze.
On edges blurred, reality bends,
In this magic, the night transcends.

The Poetry of Placement

In every spot, a tale begins,
Life breathes softly, as nature spins.
A flower blooms, a stone sits still,
Each holds purpose, each has will.

Mountains rise to kiss the sky,
Rivers carve paths, flowing by.
In gardens, in streets, there's art,
Placement whispers, speaks to the heart.

Moments linger, captured bright,
Eternal truths found in the light.
Each setting tells a story clear,
In the space we love, we persevere.

Serene Silhouettes

At dusk, the world wears soft attire,
Silhouettes against the fire.
Outlined figures dance with grace,
In the quiet, we find our place.

Mountains loom with silent pride,
Holding secrets that they hide.
Beneath the stars, we draw in breath,
In the stillness, we find depth.

Whispers echo through the night,
Guiding souls, fading light.
These serene forms, they gently sway,
In twilight's peace, we drift away.

Overhead Inspiration

In the sky, a canvas bright,
Colors dance in morning light.
Whispers of dreams take their flight,
Holding hope, hearts feel the height.

Clouds like thoughts drift and sway,
Guiding souls along their way.
With each breath, the skies convey,
Joy that blooms in the day's play.

Stars ignite the night's embrace,
In their glow, we find our place.
Every twinkle sets the pace,
For the journeys we will chase.

Let the winds of change arise,
Carrying us toward the skies.
With inspiration's gentle sighs,
Our spirits soar, and fears demise.

Cascades of Craft

Amidst the tools, creation brews,
Hands that shape, and vision cues.
Every touch tells tales anew,
Crafting worlds from hopes and hues.

With each stroke, the art unfolds,
Stories whispered, wonders told.
In the silence, passion molds,
Dreams transformed in hands so bold.

Materials dance, both wild and free,
Textures blend in harmony.
From cluttered thoughts, we start to see,
The beauty found in unity.

Let the mastery take its flight,
In the glow of day and night.
With each creation, hearts ignite,
Crafting dreams brings pure delight.

Symmetry of Senses

In balance lies a gentle tune,
Echoes dancing 'neath the moon.
Taste of sweetness, sweet perfume,
Sights that bloom in twilight's gloom.

Each heartbeat sings, a rhythmic grace,
Colors swirl in nature's space.
Textures whisper, soft embrace,
Telling tales that time can trace.

In every note, a story lives,
In every scent, a memory gives.
Touching moments, our spirit thrives,
Symmetry where life derives.

Breathe the world, embrace the light,
All our senses feel so right.
Unity in day and night,
Symmetry, our heart's delight.

Pathways to Possibility

Footsteps wander, paths untold,
Every twist, a dream to hold.
With each stride, the world unfolds,
A tapestry of life so bold.

Choices weave in the warm sun,
With open hearts, we chase our run.
Bridges built, we overcome,
Together, we become as one.

Through valleys low and mountains high,
Imagination takes to sky.
In the journey, spirits fly,
Every moment, we defy.

Let us walk where hope resides,
In every step, our future hides.
With every heartbeat as our guide,
Pathways to dreams, we'll never slide.

Stone and Story

In ancient hands, the stone awakes,
With whispered tales of time it makes.
Each chisel mark, a story told,
Of dreams encased in hues of gold.

Beneath the weight of ages past,
The echoes of the craftsman's cast.
A silent witness to the change,
In every curve, the live and strange.

A monument to love and pain,
Through weathered grace, it stands again.
To touch this art, a heart must dare,
In every stone, a world laid bare.

So when the twilight dims the sky,
The stories speak, they never die.
In stony silence, hear them sing,
The past alive, in everything.

An Architect's Daydream

Amidst the clouds, a vision blooms,
Of soaring spires and vibrant rooms.
Lines drawn in air with vision keen,
An architect's dream, a world serene.

Blueprints flutter like vibrant leaves,
In the mind's eye, the future weaves.
Colors cascade, a lively dance,
A structure born from heart's romance.

Brick by brick, the dreams arise,
Each layer holds a piece of skies.
Windows that frame the sunset glow,
In every corner, magic flows.

Thus with each draft, the dream expands,
A tapestry built with gentle hands.
And in the evening's soft embrace,
The daydream lingers, leaves its trace.

Shells of Structure

In ocean's depths, a shell unfolds,
A secret world, with stories told.
Each spiral curve, a journey vast,
A shelter born from ancient past.

Beneath the wave's embrace, they lie,
Silent guardians of the sky.
With rough and smooth, in harmony,
Nature's art, a masterpiece.

Waves caress their fragile form,
In storms, they weather, brave and warm.
Reminders of a dance with time,
In every line, a perfect rhyme.

So gather 'round, and listen close,
To whispered tales, the sea's soft prose.
In shells of structure, life persists,
A timeless bond that still exists.

Weaving the Invisible

In twilight's hush, a thread is spun,
Between the worlds, where dreams are run.
With careful hands, we stitch the night,
Creating paths of soul's delight.

Through shadows deep and light's embrace,
We weave connections, time and space.
Invisible threads that bind us tight,
A tapestry of shared insight.

With every breath, a pattern grows,
In quiet moments, love bestows.
A fabric rich, of hopes and fears,
Woven closely through the years.

So when you feel the world unwind,
Look closer still, the threads you'll find.
In every heart, the weaver's art,
Invisible ties that never part.

Structures of the Mind

In corridors of thought we roam,
Ideas rise like ancient stone.
Each echo carries dreams untold,
A palace built where memories fold.

Bridges span the gaps of fear,
Connecting whispers, bright and clear.
In shadows cast by flickering light,
We shape our visions in the night.

Rooms adorned with hopes and strife,
Crafting stories that form our life.
Within these halls, we dance and play,
Creating worlds that drift away.

Structures strong, yet fragile too,
Bound by the musings we pursue.
With every thought, a brick we lay,
Building futures from yesterday.

Threads of Creation

In the loom of time, we weave our fate,
Colors blend, and patterns create.
With each new strand, a story unfolds,
An tapestry rich with tales retold.

Threads of laughter, threads of tears,
Intertwined across the years.
Through the hands of heart and mind,
A fabric of moments, gentle and kind.

Woven dreams in patterns bright,
Guide the wanderers through the night.
With every pull, a tale begins,
As the world spins, creation spins.

Together we craft, together we grow,
In the garden where imaginations flow.
Each thread a path, a bond to keep,
In the vast tapestry of dreams we reap.

Arches of Ambition

Beneath the arches, spirits rise,
Reaching up to endless skies.
With every step, a chance we take,
Forging paths that never break.

In the shadows of towering dreams,
We carve our way through whispered schemes.
A balanced grace in every stride,
In the heart of hope, we shall abide.

Columns strong, they bear our weight,
Holding fast, defying fate.
With vision clear and purpose set,
We build the bridges not to forget.

Across these arches, futures call,
Together we stand, together we fall.
With hearts ablaze and dreams in hand,
We'll chase the light across the land.

Designs Born of Daydreams

In quiet hours, our minds take flight,
Sketching visions in soft twilight.
With every thought, a canvas grows,
A world of wonders, art that glows.

Brushes dance on palettes bright,
Colors swirl in pure delight.
Creating realms where wishes gleam,
Crafted gently from a dream.

With strokes of gold and whispers light,
We paint the canvas through the night.
In every corner, life takes shape,
A masterpiece in which we escape.

Designs like stars in evening's dome,
Call us forth to find our home.
In daydreams born, our spirits rise,
We find the magic in the skies.

Windows to the Soul

Eyes like mirrors, reflections deep,
Glimmers of secrets they silently keep.
Whispers of dreams, both gentle and bold,
Through these windows, the heart can unfold.

Soft shades of sorrow, bright beams of light,
Each glance a story, both dark and bright.
In silence they speak, emotions unmasked,
Through the windows of soul, we are unasked.

Beholding the beauty, pain and the grace,
In every gaze, we find our place.
Connecting the hearts in a world so wide,
Windows to the soul, where truths abide.

In fleeting moments, a spark ignites,
Through the windows of love, we take our flights.
Each soul, a canvas, of colors untold,
Through the windows we see, the world to behold.

Harmony in Hardship

In shadows cast by trials we face,
We find the strength to embrace the place.
In the storm's roar, a quiet sound,
Harmony whispers, resilience found.

Each burden carried brings lessons learned,
In every setback, a fire's burned.
Together we struggle, together we rise,
In hardship's embrace, the spirit flies.

Notes of sorrow blend with the cheer,
In the darkness, the light draws near.
Through pain and longing, hope can be spun,
A symphony rising, a battle won.

With every tear, a seed is sown,
From hardship's soil, new strength is grown.
In life's orchestra, we all play a part,
Harmony in hardship, the song of the heart.

Masonry of Memory

Bricks of moments laid one by one,
Stories entwined, like threads that run.
Each memory crafted with care anew,
In the masonry of life, we find our view.

Foundations of laughter, walls of our tears,
Echoes of whispers throughout the years.
Layer by layer, we build and assess,
In memories forged, we find our finesse.

Colors of joy paint the ceilings high,
While shadows of loss make us sigh.
Yet through the cracks, light still will seep,
In the masonry of memory, we keep.

A structure of love, so sturdy and bright,
With corners of hope that spark in the night.
Together we stand, in this shelter we mold,
The history written, a legacy told.

The Dance of Design

In patterns woven, a tale unfolds,
A dance of design where beauty beholds.
Curves and lines twirl in graceful embrace,
Creating a rhythm, a delicate space.

Each stitch a heartbeat, alive with intent,
In colors that whisper what words cannot meant.
The fabric of life, with textures we feel,
In this dance of design, emotions reveal.

Symmetry sways, while chaos invites,
In the dance we discover, our inner sights.
With every movement, stories entwine,
In the art of creation, our spirits align.

So let us twirl through the canvassed expanse,
Embrace the unknown, take a chance.
For in every design, a story is spun,
The dance of design, where all become one.

Archways of Reflection

In shadowed halls where whispers blend,
Memories dance like a gentle friend.
Each archway holds a story bright,
Glimmers of truth in fading light.

Beneath the stone, a secret waits,
Echoing dreams through ancient gates.
Time's passage, marked by silent cries,
In every curve, a past that lies.

The mirror's gaze reveals the soul,
Fragments of years that make us whole.
Reflections shimmer, hope and fear,
In every heart, a pathway clear.

Through archways wide, we wander free,
Seeking the paths of who we'll be.
With every step, the echoes fade,
Yet in our hearts, their music played.

Landscapes of Longing

Across the hills where shadows creep,
Silent desires awaken deep.
Fields of gold beneath the sky,
Whispers of dreams as clouds drift by.

The river flows with tales untold,
Carrying wishes, brave yet bold.
Mountains rise with a distant call,
Yearning hearts that will never fall.

Stars above in velvet night,
Hopes ignite with a million lights.
Every twinkle, a wish set free,
In landscapes vast, we long to be.

Through valleys wide, our spirits roam,
Chasing horizons, far from home.
In every breath, the ache remains,
As we traverse these tender plains.

Elements of Elysium

In gardens rich with colors bright,
Nature's song sings of pure delight.
Each petal soft, each breeze a kiss,
Moments crafted in tranquil bliss.

Waterfalls whisper secrets clear,
Echoing laughter, drawing near.
The sun dips low, painting the sky,
A canvas vast where dreams can fly.

Mountains stand like ancient guards,
Cradling peace in their mighty yards.
With every leaf and every stone,
The essence of Elysium is shown.

In this realm where harmony sways,
We find the light in golden rays.
Each breath we take, a gift divine,
In elements pure, our hearts align.

Paving the Poetic Path

With every word, a step begins,
Crafting tales where magic spins.
Ink upon the silent page,
Journey starts, a wise old sage.

Through valleys deep and mountains high,
Lines unfold, like birds that fly.
Each stanza builds a bridge of dreams,
Flowing gently like sunlit streams.

The rhythm guides our wandering souls,
As verses dance and boldly strolls.
In every thought, a path laid bare,
Poetic whispers fill the air.

Together we tread this sacred ground,
In every heartbeat, art is found.
Paving stones of love and truth,
The stories flourish, age of youth.

Sentinels of Shape

In shadows cast by ancient stone,
The builders mark their claims alone.
Each chisel bite, each careful strike,
Transforms the mundane into the hike.

Guardians stand at corners tight,
Embodying dreams in silent night.
Their whispers weave through time and space,
Defining realms with sacred grace.

With hands of earth and minds of fire,
They mold the world, fuel its desire.
Beneath their watch, life takes its form,
In every curve, a new norm.

Through rafters high and walls so bold,
Their stories of creation unfold.
The sentinels of shape will stay,
As time erases all in play.

Psalms of the Blueprint

Lines and angles dance with fate,
On paper scripts, we contemplate.
Sketches flow with whispered tone,
A symphony of stone on stone.

Every mark, a heartbeat drawn,
Each detail shines with gentle dawn.
In every space, the future speaks,
Knowledge built in humble peaks.

Psalms of structure, hymns of hope,
Crafted dreams, a boundless scope.
Plans unfold like pages bright,
Guiding hands in day and night.

From vision born, to form embraced,
Blueprints nurture the dreams we've chased.
Keys to realms yet yet undefined,
In each design, our souls aligned.

Dreams on the Drafting Table

Upon the wood, ideas collide,
Where passion flows and thoughts reside.
Drafted lines of futures sought,
In every stroke, a lesson taught.

Markers dance in brilliant hues,
Sketching paths that we might choose.
With every curve, a tale begins,
In quiet moments, a world spins.

Layouts bloom like spring's first rose,
Concepts breathe, then take repose.
Each design, a fleeting chance,
To craft the world, to dream a dance.

The drafting table holds our hopes,
In measured space, our spirit copes.
With open hearts and eyes that gleam,
We sketch the life of every dream.

The Aperture of Ambition

Through a lens, a vision clear,
Ambition beckons, drawing near.
With focused gaze and steady hand,
We navigate this promised land.

The world unfolds in frames of light,
Each shuttered moment ignites the night.
In pursuit of dreams, we boldly tread,
Awake in visions, not just in bed.

The aperture opens wide and bold,
Capturing tales yet to be told.
In every click, our story grows,
Mapping paths that life bestows.

With each click and every sigh,
Chasing shadows that drift and fly.
Ambition's flame, an endless spark,
Guides us forth from light to dark.

Sketches of Serenity

In quiet mornings, soft winds flow,
Leaves dance gently, a soothing show.
The sun peeks in with warm embrace,
Nature whispers, a sacred space.

Calm streams murmur, secrets untold,
Stories of peace in ripples unfold.
Birds take flight, tracing the skies,
In their freedom, deep solace lies.

A canvas painted in hues of blue,
Each stroke breathes calm, a tranquil view.
Moments linger, lost in time,
In this stillness, hearts gently chime.

Evening falls, stars brightly gleam,
Moonlight weaves through a soft, silver dream.
With open hearts, we breathe the night,
In the silence, we find our light.

The Anatomy of Aspirations

In every heartbeat, dreams ignite,
Sparked by hope, shining so bright.
Chasing shadows, weaving our paths,
Unraveling fate, embracing the laughs.

Climbing mountains, scaling the heights,
Facing fears, turning wrongs into rights.
With whispers of courage, we move ahead,
Fueled by visions that dance in our head.

Each step forward, a story unfolds,
Crafted in passion, embraced in bolds.
We sketch our lives with shadows and light,
A tapestry woven of day and night.

Fingers trace futures, subtly inked,
In every moment, aspirations linked.
Together we rise, together we stand,
In the anatomy of dreams, hand in hand.

Canvases of Structure

Brick by brick, the foundation grows,
Crafting spaces where passion flows.
Architects of dreams, we build and shape,
In blueprints, our visions escape.

Lines and angles, precise and true,
Every corner hides stories anew.
Structures rise, reaching for skies,
In their shadows, our spirit flies.

Paint splatters, an artist's delight,
Coloring visions that dance with light.
Each canvas holds the potential within,
A place where creation and life begin.

With every hammer, we sing our song,
In melodies of steel, we belong.
Canvases of structure, strong and grand,
Holding hopes and dreams in our hands.

Shadows in the Studio

In the studio, shadows play,
Dancing figures, night meets day.
Brushes stroke, whispers abound,
In every corner, creativity found.

Easel standing, poised and still,
Capturing moments, time to fulfill.
Canvas waiting, dreams to ignite,
In this sacred space, we take flight.

Palette rich, colors collide,
In the murmur of art, we confide.
Shadows weave through the gentle light,
Guiding the heart through artistic night.

With every layer, stories unfold,
Crafting memories in shades of bold.
In shadows' embrace, we find our way,
In the studio, we forever stay.

Foundations of Dreams

In the quiet air, whispers rise,
Seeds of hope in endless skies.
With each step, we pave the way,
To light the path of a new day.

Brick by brick, we build our fate,
Crafting futures, we recreate.
In shadows cast, the visions grow,
From the heart, the dreams will flow.

With open minds and open hearts,
We gather strength, ignite the sparks.
In the temple of our fears,
We forge a world that perseveres.

Let courage guide the sculptor's hand,
As dreams emerge, we take a stand.
Foundations laid, we rise as one,
In the dance of life, we have begun.

Visions in Stone

Chiseled forms in the fading light,
Echoes of dreams, bold and bright.
Carved from silence, the stories unfold,
In the heart of the stone, secrets told.

Hands of artisans shape the clay,
Molding whispers from yesterday.
Fragments of time, preserved in grace,
Each sculpture tells of a hidden place.

As shadows dance on rugged stone,
Visions awaken, claiming their throne.
The past and present intertwine,
In every curve, the stars align.

From mountain peaks to ocean's call,
Nature's wonders, we feel them all.
In stone we find our hopes embraced,
Visions alive, forever traced.

The Craft of Creation

In the workshop where dreams ignite,
Hands at work, minds taking flight.
Every tool sings a song so sweet,
As visions blend in rhythmic beat.

Colors splash on canvas white,
Imagination's pure delight.
With every stroke, the story grows,
A tapestry of highs and lows.

From the fire, the metal bends,
Crafting beauty that transcends.
Through patience, the artist's grace,
In every piece, a sacred space.

The world awakens to creation's call,
Artistry that connects us all.
In the craft, we find our place,
United by this endless chase.

Edges of Imagination

In the corners where dreams reside,
Imagination's whispers collide.
A canvas stretched beyond the mind,
Where the wildest thoughts unwind.

Curves and angles, undefined,
In shadows deep, new worlds we find.
Each line drawn, a story's start,
With every leap, we break apart.

Across dimensions, we boldly soar,
Exploring realms we've yet to explore.
Boundless spirit, a guiding light,
In the edges, we meet the night.

From dreams to life, a fragile thread,
In this dance, we will not dread.
The journey calls, with vibrant schemes,
At the edges, we weave our dreams.

Heights of Harmony

In the whisper of the breeze,
Where the songbirds sing with ease,
Mountains echo joy and cheer,
Nature's pulse, forever near.

Clouds drift by in soft embrace,
Painting skies, a tranquil space,
Sunset warms the evening glow,
In this peace, our spirits flow.

Stars emerge, like dreams in flight,
Guiding hearts through velvet night,
In the heights, we find our voice,
In connection, we rejoice.

Harmony in every sound,
In this place, true love is found,
Together, hand in hand we tread,
On this path where pure hearts led.

Archways of Aspiration

Through the arches, dreams arise,
Where ambition meets the skies,
Steps of courage, bold and bright,
Chasing visions, pure delight.

Each doorway opens, paths to take,
A journey formed, a leap we make,
In the shadows, light will gleam,
Leading us toward our dream.

With each threshold, we believe,
In ourselves, we can achieve,
Voices whisper, futures call,
In this space, we stand tall.

Together, building what we seek,
With every word, and every peak,
Archways rise to greet the dawn,
In this spirit, we move on.

Dreams Beneath the Surface

In quiet depths where shadows play,
Lies a world both dark and gray,
Whispers linger, secrets told,
In the depths, our dreams unfold.

Echoes splash like distant waves,
In the quiet, hope still braves,
Glimmers shine in hidden air,
Lessons learned from depths we dare.

Beneath the surface, truths reside,
Pulling gently, like the tide,
In the stillness, visions gleam,
Beneath it all, we weave our dream.

Through the layers, we will dive,
Finding ways to stay alive,
In this journey, hearts remain,
A tapestry of joy and pain.

Canvas of Construction

On the easel, dreams are splayed,
Colors blend in bright array,
Brush in hand, the vision starts,
Crafting tales from open hearts.

With each stroke, a story flows,
Building worlds that everyone knows,
Textures blend, emotions rise,
A dance of light beneath the skies.

Layers deepen with the time,
Every hue, a whisper's rhyme,
In this space, our souls reside,
As we build, we do not hide.

From chaos comes a masterpiece,
In creation, we find peace,
With the dawn, our wishes bloom,
On this canvas, we find room.

Spirals of Thought

In the quiet night, thoughts unwind,
Echoes of dreams, softly entwined.
Whispers of wisdom, flutter and flee,
Dancing like leaves from a wise old tree.

Questions arise like smoke in the air,
Lacing the dark with threads of despair.
Yet hope flickers on like a distant star,
Guiding the lost, no matter how far.

Chasing the spiral, I search for the light,
Finding my way through a tapestry bright.
Each twist and turn, a lesson I learn,
In spirals of thought, I continue to yearn.

So here I will stay, with my musings in flow,
Tracing the patterns, both high and low.
In this endless dance of mind and of heart,
Spirals of thought, they will never depart.

Pillars of Passion

In the heart of the fire, where dreams take form,
Burns a radiant flame, an artist's norm.
Crafted from love, each shadow and light,
Pillars of passion rise, bold and bright.

With every heartbeat, a rhythm is found,
Crafting the echoes, a powerful sound.
Each stroke of the brush, each note of the song,
Pillars of passion, where we all belong.

Through valleys of doubt, we stand tall and sure,
With flames in our hearts, forever we endure.
Fusing our spirits, through struggles we climb,
Pillars of passion, transcending all time.

In every endeavor, we forge what we seek,
The strength of our dreams, the will to be unique.
Together we rise, our voices in motion,
Pillars of passion, a boundless devotion.

Curves of Creativity

Let the lines meander, in soft gentle waves,
Creating new pathways, where inspiration paves.
Colors collide, in a dance so divine,
Curves of creativity, gracefully align.

In the chaos of life, where shapes may distort,
Art finds a way, in playful consort.
With laughter and joy, we sketch and we draw,
Curves of creativity, open the door.

Ideas spin wildly, like leaves in the breeze,
Whirling and twirling, with effortless ease.
In the garden of thoughts, we plant every seed,
Curves of creativity, fulfilling our need.

So let us embrace, the unusual flow,
For in each curve lies the room to grow.
Through art and through heart, we mold and we bend,
Curves of creativity, where all paths transcend.

Sanctuary of Shadows

In the hush of night, secrets reside,
Whispering softly, where shadows abide.
Beneath the pale moon, in silence we find,
Sanctuary of shadows, a refuge for mind.

With every heartbeat, the darkness unfolds,
Stories untold, in the silence, it molds.
Glimmers of hope, woven through night,
Sanctuary of shadows, in comfort, we write.

Here in the stillness, our fears take flight,
Dancing in corners, evading the light.
A place of reflection, where dreams intertwine,
Sanctuary of shadows, a haven divine.

In the depths of the night, we gather our dreams,
Finding our strengths, in the quietest beams.
Embracing the dark, as our fears start to show,
Sanctuary of shadows, where we all can grow.

Foundations of Wonder

In the cradle of night, stars sing,
Dreams unfurl like wings in the sky.
Whispers of magic, secrets they bring,
Eyes aglow with the questions that fly.

Beneath the surface, the river flows,
Ancient stories in currents reside.
Each pebble an echo, a tale that grows,
In the dance of the shadows, truth cannot hide.

Mountains high, valleys deep,
Nature's canvas, colors collide.
Inspiring visions, the heart will keep,
Boundless worlds where wonders abide.

Every moment a spark, a divine chance,
To explore the unknown, daring and free.
Join the journey, join the dance,
Foundations of wonder, our spirits agree.

Emblems of Existence

Life's fleeting moments, captured in time,
Emblems of existence, fragile yet bold.
Each heartbeat a rhythm, a silent rhyme,
In the tapestry woven, our stories unfold.

The sun's gentle touch on the morning dew,
A reminder, a promise of warmth we find.
In laughter and sorrow, the shades of hue,
Emblems of existence, beautifully intertwined.

In the dance of the leaves, the whispering breeze,
Nature's symphony plays, a vibrant score.
Every heartbeat echoes, moments to seize,
Emblems of existence, forever we explore.

With every sunrise, new paths to tread,
In the shadows of doubt, courage will rise.
In love's tender embrace, the heart is fed,
Emblems of existence, painted in the skies.

Heights of Hope

In the stillness of dawn, a whisper glows,
Hope blooms softly, like petals in spring.
Rising from ashes, the spirit grows,
A promise of light, on the winds of a fling.

Mountains await, their peaks gleam bright,
Each step a journey, toward dreams untold.
Above the clouds, where the heart takes flight,
Heights of hope beckon, fierce and bold.

When shadows creep close, and doubts crowd the mind,
Hold fast to the dreams that spark in the dark.
Together we'll venture, no soul left behind,
In the heights of hope, we'll ignite the spark.

Across the horizons, where visions align,
With courage as compass, we'll chase the sun.
In unity's embrace, our spirits entwine,
Heights of hope promise, we've only begun.

Interfaces of Insight

In the quietest moments, wisdom reveals,
Interfaces of insight, where thoughts intertwine.
Fragments of truth in the silence, it feels,
Guiding the lost back to pathways divine.

Through the lens of the heart, we begin to see,
Connections so subtle, yet wondrously clear.
Each glance a reflection, the spirit set free,
Interfaces of insight pull us near.

In the labyrinth of thoughts, we wander and roam,
A map drawn by questions that lead us to grace.
In every encounter, we find a new home,
Interfaces of insight, life's intricate lace.

The answers we seek, in the stillness reside,
In whispers of reason, they gently arrive.
With open hearts, we stand side by side,
Interfaces of insight, where we come alive.

Forming Fantasies

In shadows dance the dreams we weave,
Threads of light in twilight's leave.
Hearts painted with vibrant hues,
Awake, alive, chasing what we choose.

Whispers echo in the night,
Crafting visions, pure delight.
With every sigh, a story spun,
A tapestry 'neath the silver sun.

Endless realms, horizons blend,
In the fabric, we transcend.
Laughter lingers, sweet and free,
Forming fantasies, you and me.

As dawn breaks with gentle grace,
Our hopes emerge, embrace the chase.
Together here, we'll always dream,
In this world, where all is gleam.

Spaces Between Thoughts

In quiet moments, silence speaks,
Nestled deep where stillness leaks.
Between the beats of heart and mind,
A realm of peace, so hard to find.

Floating softly like whispering air,
Dancing lightly without a care.
Ideas linger, ebb and flow,
In this sanctuary, revelations grow.

Glimmers of insight, fleeting light,
Shadows linger just out of sight.
In the pauses, wisdom hides,
Spaces between, where meaning resides.

A profound stillness, time suspends,
Listening closely, the journey bends.
To find ourselves in what's not seen,
In spaces between, we grow serene.

Geometry of the Heart

Shapes collide in patterns bright,
Angles twist, revealing light.
In every curve, a rhythm flows,
Mapping love in silent prose.

Lines that guide, connect our souls,
Intersecting paths, we reach our goals.
Triangles form, a stable base,
Foundations strong, in love's embrace.

Circles endless, always near,
In unity, we share our fear.
Each quadrant holds a truth untold,
A geometry that never grows old.

The heart's designs, a sacred plan,
Drawn together, hand in hand.
In every angle, every part,
Lies the beauty—the geometry of the heart.

Facades of Imagination

Behind the masks, our dreams reside,
Whispers of worlds we cannot hide.
Colors clash in bold display,
Facades shift as night turns day.

In woven tales, we craft our fate,
Shadows dance as we create.
Each layer adds a mystic charm,
Reality bends without alarm.

Echoes of fantasies take flight,
Hiding truths in the dead of night.
Mirrors reflect what we can't see,
Facades of imagination set us free.

Through painted skies and vibrant dreams,
Illusions swirl in silver beams.
In every heart, a story waits,
Behind the facades, destiny creates.

Tapestry of Vision

Threads of light weave in the air,
Colors dance, they have no care.
Dreams unfurl in vibrant hues,
Creating paths we dare to choose.

Glimmers spark in twilight's gaze,
Whispers echo through the maze.
Each strand tells a tale unique,
In every knot, a secret speak.

Woven hearts beat with the breeze,
Nature's brush paints with such ease.
Every vision finds its place,
Entwined in time, we leave our trace.

As dawn awakens, threads will shine,
A tapestry weaved, truly divine.
Every moment stitched with care,
In this art, our souls lay bare.

Echoes of Elegance

Softly glows the evening light,
Whispers float in gentle night.
Every sound a sweet embrace,
In this place, we find our grace.

Pavements shine with silent pride,
Graceful steps as dreams collide.
With every breath, our spirits soar,
In elegance, we crave for more.

Echoes dance from hill to vale,
Stories woven in the trail.
Timeless beauty lingers long,
In the heart, we hear the song.

As stars adorn the velvet sky,
We find solace in the high.
Through cherishing, we embrace,
These echoes of our sacred space.

Geometry of Emotion

Shapes arise in heart's domain,
Lines connect in joy and pain.
Angles sharp, yet soft embrace,
In this form, we find our place.

Circles draw the endless flow,
Infinite, like love's true glow.
Triangles stand with strength and might,
In their lines, we seek the light.

Squares of memory fine and true,
Hold the dreams we once knew.
Symmetry of laughter bright,
Guides us through the darkest night.

With each curve, each point, each line,
In this geometry, we shine.
Crafting feelings, bold and pure,
In emotion, we endure.

The Art of Ascent

One step leads to heights unknown,
With each breath, the spirit's grown.
Mountains call with siren's song,
In their arms, we all belong.

Pathways twist, the air is thin,
Yet within us, the fire's twin.
Heartbeats echo with each stride,
In the journey, dreams abide.

Clouds wrap gently 'round our quest,
Every summit holds its best.
Views that stretch beyond the eye,
In this reach, we learn to fly.

With each venture, we ascend,
Finding peace where skies extend.
In the art, we craft our fate,
Onward, upward, never wait.

The Art of Edifices

In stone and steel, a tale unfolds,
Crafted dreams in frames that hold.
Each line a whisper, a secret cast,
In shadows long, their stories last.

Balconies sigh with tales of time,
Where laughter danced, a fleeting rhyme.
Windows glance at worlds beyond,
In arches proud, our hearts respond.

From roots in earth, to skies above,
These structures breathe, they pulse with love.
We trace our fingers on the walls,
In every crack, a memory calls.

With every brick, a vision sown,
In every curve, a feeling grown.
The art of edifices stands tall,
A testament to dreams, for one and all.

Echoes in Empty Spaces

Within the silence, whispers hide,
In vacant rooms, where dreams abide.
Each echo tells a story lost,
Of laughter shared and hearts embossed.

The walls can hold a breathless pause,
An absent sound that sings its cause.
In corners dark, a shadow plays,
A haunting waltz of faded days.

Beneath the beams, the thoughts collide,
What once was bright now must reside.
The air is thick with things unsaid,
In empty spaces, hopes are fed.

A fragile peace in silence found,
Within these bounds, the soul unbound.
Echoes linger, soft and deep,
In hollow hearts, their secrets keep.

Visions in the Vault

Glimmers shine where darkness yields,
In vaulted dreams, our fate reveals.
Through arches wide, the light cascades,
Unveiling paths where hope pervades.

The ceiling high, a canvas bare,
Each stroke of thought, a breath of air.
With every glance, a world appears,
In whispered tones, our fate endears.

We reach for stars in open skies,
Beneath the vault, the spirit flies.
In every shadow, visions dwell,
A sacred space where dreams compel.

The heartbeat echoes, strong and bright,
In sacred halls, we chase the light.
Visions soar beyond the stone,
In this grand vault, we find our home.

Columns of Creativity

In columns strong, ideas rise,
Like ancient trees beneath the skies.
Support for dreams that sway and bend,
In creativity, we make amends.

Each pillar tells a tale divine,
Of moments lost and future shine.
A tapestry of thoughts unfurled,
In every column, a new world.

With open hearts, we gather near,
To share our visions, free from fear.
Together we build, a strong design,
In columns bold, our tales entwine.

Let laughter spill and colors blend,
In this embrace, our hearts extend.
For in our craft, we find the key,
In columns of creativity.